CONTENTS

Winter Survival

Winter can be a cruel, harsh, and unforgiving season. Snow may cover the land, making both travel and the finding of food and water difficult for many animals. Freezing temperatures can rob bodies of heat essential to life, but most species seem to have developed their own strategies for winter survival.

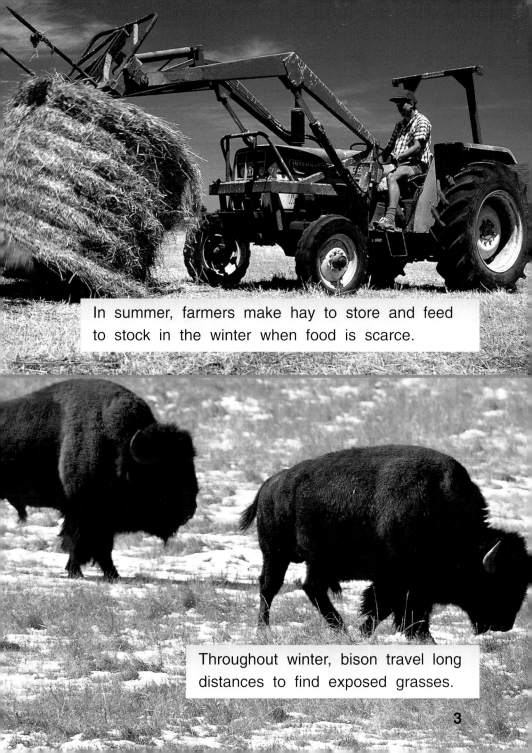

In summer, farmers make hay to store and feed to stock in the winter when food is scarce.

Throughout winter, bison travel long distances to find exposed grasses.

FALLING TEMPERATURES

Temperatures begin to fall in the early autumn. Deciduous trees with broad leaves respond to the shorter days and cooler nights with displays of vibrant autumn colours. The falling temperatures and the autumn frosts are first noticed by the creatures living in the mountains.

In autumn, monarch butterflies "fuel up" on pollen in the Allegheny Mountains in Pennsylvania before taking off on a 4,800-kilometre flight to Mexico for the winter.

Ptarmigans blend into the autumn foliage. Before winter comes, their plumage will turn to white, protecting them from predators.

WINTER PREPARATIONS

During the autumn months, animals that hibernate fatten up on food. Throughout the long months of winter, hibernating animals convert their body fat into energy to stay warm. Their heart rate slows down to conserve energy.

Cold-blooded salamanders survive the winter by hibernating beneath the frozen surface of ponds.

This grizzly bear is fattening up on autumn berries. In its winter den, the hibernating grizzly will convert fat into energy. It uses the energy to keep itself warm.

STORING AND SAVING

Some animals survive winter by living off stores of saved food that they hoarded throughout the autumn in burrows and hollow trees. During cold winter days, they will sleep a lot and feed from their stores, but on sunny winter days they leave their homes to hunt for extra food and sun themselves.

In the autumn, tree squirrels collect and store more nuts than they can eat. Nut caches will feed them during winter months when the trees are bare.

In Athabasca, Alaska, people dry salmon and store it for winter days when food is more difficult to find.

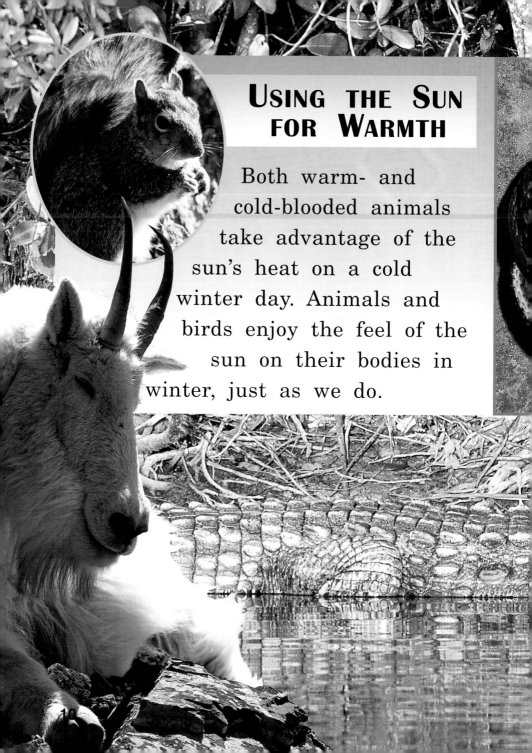

USING THE SUN FOR WARMTH

Both warm- and cold-blooded animals take advantage of the sun's heat on a cold winter day. Animals and birds enjoy the feel of the sun on their bodies in winter, just as we do.

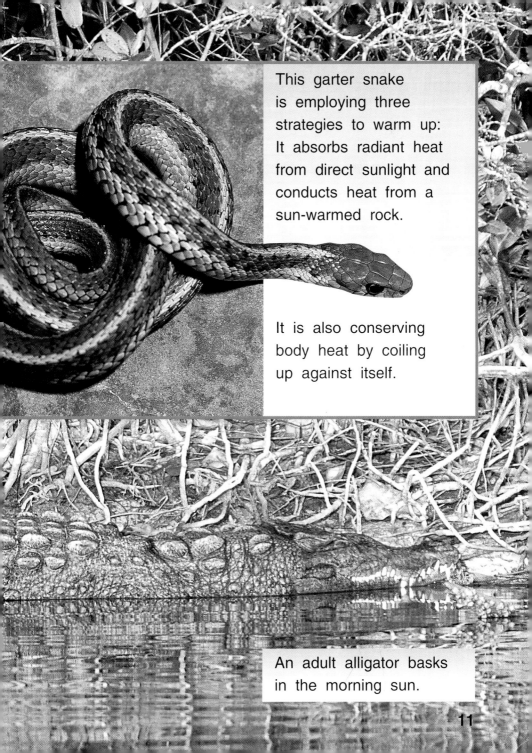

This garter snake is employing three strategies to warm up: It absorbs radiant heat from direct sunlight and conducts heat from a sun-warmed rock.

It is also conserving body heat by coiling up against itself.

An adult alligator basks in the morning sun.

11

WINTER COATS

Staying warm is essential to survival. Warm-blooded animals must insulate their bodies from chilly winter temperatures. Mammals have fur, which retains body heat. A fur coat traps air next to the body, just as a winter jacket traps air next to your body.

White fur blends into a snow-covered world to protect the owner from wolves searching for a meal.

A polar bear naps on frozen snow and ice. A thick winter coat and a layer of body fat provide insulation.

SNUGGLING FOR WARMTH

Snuggling is a special strategy used by many species, including the human species, to stay warm. By snuggling together, animals can share each other's body warmth. They will also snuggle unprotected noses or beaks into their bodies, in the same way we snuggle our hands up our sleeves.

MIGRATION

Seasonal migration is a special survival strategy used by many creatures. By travelling to lands with plentiful food supplies in the summer and then retreating to the warmer areas for the winter, some species have the best of both worlds.

Polar bears make a solitary migration north to the frozen Arctic seas to hunt seals.

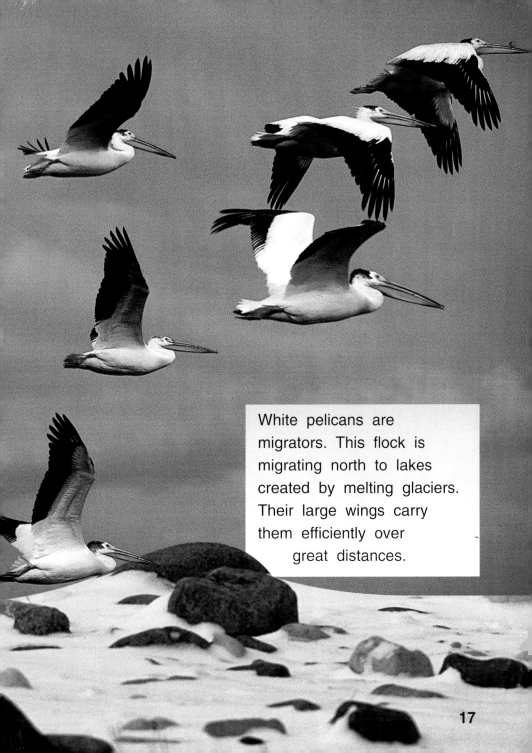

White pelicans are migrators. This flock is migrating north to lakes created by melting glaciers. Their large wings carry them efficiently over great distances.

17

SAFETY IN NUMBERS

Most migrating animals travel in flocks or herds. This gives migrators several advantages over travelling alone. One advantage is that there is some safety in big numbers against the many predators. But the best advantage might be that the younger animals can follow a leader who knows how to find its way!

When winter comes, bighorn sheep migrate to lower altitudes.

Elk travel the same migration routes to their winter ranges every year. There, they find grass to graze on without the worry of deep snows.

Migrating elk travel in herds to the winter range. As spring approaches, the herds will return to their mountain home.

19

SPRING APPROACHES

As the streams and lakes begin to thaw, the migrators start returning to their summer habitats. Patches of green grass begin to appear through the snow and, once again, animals can find food and water more easily. Thick winter coats are shed. Winter is over for another year.

Grasshoppers die at the first autumn frost. Eggs, laid before the frosts, survive the winter to hatch in spring.

As spring comes, bison gorge on the fresh green grass.

INDEX

ABOUT BUCK WILDE

box 16 Ketchum, id 83340

Observers of wildlife can often stress wild animals – especially during harsh winter months. When I was shooting the photographs for my book *Winter Survival*, I had to be careful that my presence didn't cause any animals to abandon a food source that might be vital for their survival.

The winter environment was also challenging for me as a photographer. My fingers and toes were frequently chilled by sub-zero temperatures. The batteries for my camera didn't last very long and my cameras and lenses would have frozen if I hadn't handled them carefully. My film also became brittle and very hard to handle.

The advice I give to all young photographers is "to take pictures of wildlife in the warmer, friendlier months". It's easier on your subjects, your camera gear, and your fingers and toes.

Written by **Buck Wilde**
Photographed by **Buck Wilde**
Edited by **Sue Ledington**
Designed by **Amanda Gordon**
Photographic research by **Sarah Irvine**

Additional photography by **Ant Photo Library:** Dave Watts (pygmy possum hibernating, p. 6); **Hedgehog House:** John Eastcott (child, p. 12); Colin Monteath (husky sleeping, p. 14); **N.Z. Picture Library:** (p. 15); **Photobank:** (making hay, p. 3; cows, p. 14)

02 01 00 99 98 97
10 9 8 7 6 5 4 3 2 1

Published by Shortland Publications Limited, 2B Cawley Street, Ellerslie, Auckland, New Zealand
Distributed in Australia by Rigby Heinemann, a division of Reed International Books Australia Pty Ltd. ACN 001 002 357, 22 Salmon Street, Port Melbourne, Victoria 3207
Distributed in the United Kingdom by Kingscourt Publishing Limited, P.O. Box 1427, Freepost, London W6 9BR

Printed by Colorcraft, Hong Kong
ISBN: 0-7901-1687-1